Life's Journey

Latrivia Brown

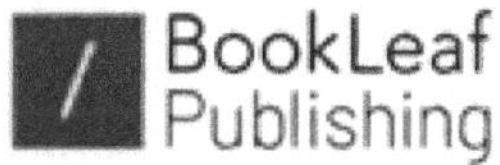

BookLeaf
Publishing

Presentation by *BookLeaf Publishing*

Web: www.bookleafpub.com

E-mail: info@bookleafpub.com

ISBN: 9789357210911

First edition 2022

DEDICATION

Taegenae,

 I wish you were here to read this just know that you are my total inspiration for everything I've done lately.

I love & miss you 12/11/2001-06/20/2021

The Beat Don't Stop

ACKNOWLEDGEMENT

Curley, Tadagenae, Taegenae & Tahlayja
without you all my life would have been totally
different. I am who I am because of you 4. I
strive daily to be a better mom and woman so
you guys can see that in life growth is
continuous. I just want you all to know that I
Love you and only want the best for you all.

Zacharias & Cartier my gambabies and my
second chances I Love y'all

Mom & Dad without you both I would not be
here thank you for life and not giving up on me I
strive to be a better as an adult than I was as a
child I know your grey hairs came from me lol
just know that I love you both

Andresha my sister Thank You for always being
there for me nothing in this world can replace
the bond that we have I Love You and proud of
the woman you became

Koolie I truly appreciate you Thanks for being a
good listener when I'm on my rants and thanks
for supporting my many endeavors including
this one "to be or not to be" lol I love you

PREFACE

What ever life brings be the greatest YOU

Faith

Believing in something you have not seen
hoping that it will indeed come to fruition
frequently tested by obstacles trials and
tribulations are constant reminders that you need
to have Faith eventually you get all that you
hoped for if you don't loose site of your faith

Love

LOVE
Is Gentle
Waking up when you rather sleep
Is selfless
Putting yourself last when others need to be first
Is forgiving
Growing past FLAWS and SHORTCOMINGS
Is honesty
Telling the TRUTH even when it HURTS
Is the most misused word in the dictionary
LOVE

Beautiful Pretender

3

What a beautiful pretender you are
You walk around saying everything someone
wants to hear but your actions proves different.
Beautiful pretender!! Each day it's a new show
because all you're doing is acting. I want to see
what's real and true about you. All I can see and
smell is the fake you portray. Who are you
really?
I see you as a pretender and don't know how to
deal with you or how to treat the situations that
arise daily. You act as if it's nothing you believe
your own lies or do you make your own truths? I
can tell you March to your own beat! do you
even have a heart for others around you?
Beautiful Pretender is what you are.....

Giving Up

Things may get rough at times.
Your life may seem like its in shambles; day in and day out.
It might feel like everything is falling apart. You lost yourself in a marriage, as a parent, a friend; it seems like there is no way back to who you once were. No one seems to understand nor care about what you are going through. WE DO! Pull yourself together second by second if that's what it takes. Those seconds will soon become minutes and minutes will be hours. That will soon turn into days. YOU! Yes YOU! Are still here for a purpose! YOU will make it! YOU will fulfill all your dreams! It takes YOU to stand up and START
GIVING UP IS NOT AN OPTION

Bloom

The seed was planted with passion
Nine months of bliss
Six months of sleepless nights
Two years of becoming a track star
Five years of pure amazement
Ten years of pride and joy
Fifteen oh what happened to my baby
Twenty years of those sleepless nights again
Twenty Five years at awe of the growth and
transformation

Marriage

When you decided to get married you had forever in mind so why are you letting trials and tribulations change what you originally planned it to be no one ever said it would be easy so take a step back and remember how you felt on your wedding day and why you said I do to begin with

Young Adult

I know everything
Do not help me
I blame my parents for everything thats wrong
Fix it fast
I'll just throw it away and get another one
I don't want to work
I rather hang out with my friends
I'm not going to be like you
I'll own a home by the time I'm 25
Generation

Parenting

There's no Manuel or special book that can prepare you for it with one child or twenty children every experience will be different you will learn cry laugh worry and probably pray along the way there will be easy days and hard ones too but don't you dare give up on them they are part of you

Grief

No day is the same There's no timeline emotions
are all over the place keeping busy doesn't help
when all you can think of is what your loved one
is missing or would have been doing it is
something you can not prepare for its said to be
a part of life you just deal and continue to LIVE

Super Hero

For my Super Hero:
As I look into your eyes I am mesmerized by the
soft brown tone and the glistening spark that
leads to your heart

If I look deep enough I see your fears and tears it
appears that your soul is crying yet dying to be
captured by an external love that's pure as a dove
and Loyal as a an owl

The outer parts of your being Is so strong and
tantalizing yet your bold brown eyes shows just
how much this world has become your
cryptonite even with all your might those
beautiful eyes shows the true story that's inside

Beyond your outter layer of steel they're
showing the core of your hearts desires

Your eyes leads to the heart that wants to love
and be loved
Stop looking up and looking out your one true
love has already been found...............

Destined to be

Forever isn't long enough for this type of love once our souls met it didn't matter how far apart we were or long it took to reconnect we was destined to be one I still get butterflies when I look into your eyes I still blush when you walk into the room Your kisses makes time stop my heart race and my body melt Your touch takes me to a place of no return the sound of your voice send vibrations through my veins to my heart there is comfort in the way you hold me I'm in a constant dream where time has lapsed and I see clear visions of us in our 70's still skipping to the same beat

Steps in life

12

Forgive
 Learn
  Love yourself
   Be Selfless
    Set Goals
     Don't Give Up
      Repeat

Loosing a child

13

The hardest thing in life a parent can endure our greatest fear from conception til the day it happens no matter the age or situation you will not be prepared for the turmoil within that follows you wanted your child to be there to live a long fulfilling life the hurt and pain is unbearable at times the question will always remain WHY MY CHILD not one person can answer it

Happiness

Its found within you no person place or thing
can make you happy you will continue to search
for happiness until you fully understand that it
has always been in you

Forgiveness

Forgiveness

When its all said and done its for you

           Forgiveness

Time

Lost in transition every moment counts its valuable and expensive to lose it is wasted taken for granted missed opportunities occupied by memories and lessons use it wisely you'll never get it back

Your Time

Peer Pressure

Peer Pressure cost you your life you do things against your better judgement drinking doing drugs having sex getting into relationships prematurely you tend to tolerate behaviors that normally wouldn't be ok you find yourself in awkward situations you constantly tell yourself you are better than this but continue to adjust to the lifestyle of others to fit in what's sad some are 15 trying to figure it all out and others are over 50 and should already have it figured out

Imperfect Happily Ever After

Nobody is perfect

If you want to spend an imperfect happily ever after where we are aware of our flaws and imperfections and strive to be better as one we can ignore the influences of the world on what we should be

And just do it

Nineteen

19

19 was your number funny thing is I had you at
19 never could I imagine that after 19 years of
love 19 years of memories 19 years of fighting
19 years of triumphs 19 years of life we would
be saying goodbye to such a beautiful soul

A true friend

One of the most important relationships you will have throughout life once you have a real friend you will know the bond will be different your true friend will tell you when you are right and let you no if you are wrong true friends will not lead you in the wrong direction they love you as a sister/brother so your life matters to a true friend the bond of a true friend is unmatched you can speak everyday or once a year and it will always be the same true friends understand that you have a life outside of them and will not require all of your time

Life & Death

21

Everyday you should be learning the day
you stop learning you have died like a
sun flower without sunlight

www.ingramcontent.com/pod-product-compliance
Lightning Source LLC
Chambersburg PA
CBHW070733160726
48003CB00006BA/2481